CHHATRAPATI
THE LEGACY

Ukiyoto Publishing

All global publishing rights are held by

Ukiyoto Publishing

Published in 2025

Content Copyright © Ukiyoto

ISBN 9789364949989

All rights reserved.

No part of this publication may be reproduced, transmitted, or stored in a retrieval system, in any form by any means, electronic, mechanical, photocopying, recording or otherwise, without the prior permission of the publisher.

The moral rights of the author have been asserted.

This book is sold subject to the condition that it shall not by way of trade or otherwise, be lent, resold, hired out or otherwise circulated, without the publisher's prior consent, in any form of binding or cover other than that in which it is published.

www.ukiyoto.com

Contents

The Code of Chivalry *By Kajari Guha*	1
Chhatrapati Shivaji Maharaj who Dreamt Swarajya *By Aurobindo Ghosh*	9
Shivaji, the Maratha Legend *By Devajit Bhuyan*	21
A Dream That Came True *By Priyadarshi Ravi*	33
The Living Legacy *By Dr Priyanka Joshi*	39
Chhatrapati-The Legacy *By Rohan Narvekar*	44
Beyond Borders: A Love That Defied Tradition *By Manmohan Sadana*	57
Revelations of the Deccan *By Anay Saxena*	63
About the Authors	*71*

The Code of Chivalry

By Kajari Guha

Preface

Chatrapati Shivaji Maharaj, the founder of the Maratha Empire, in the 17 the century, challenged the Mughal and Adil Shahi rule. Besides being a brilliant military strategist and a great administrator, Shivaji had high regards for women. He rescued women from enemy camps and personally ensured justice for women who were mistreated. He had equal respect for women who belonged to different backgrounds, regardless of caste, creed and religion. He encouraged the women's role in society. He buoyed up women to participate in governance and administration.

The protagonist of my story is a young man who rescued a young girl from the clutches of the family that tried to exploit her.

Story

Finally, Punni was all alone in her dark damp poorly lit room. This attic was the only place where she could be all on her own after the day's drudgery.

"Punni! Wash my clothes that I have kept in my closet. Then press them after they get dried. Tomorrow I need them urgently." Rumi, the pampered young daughter of Dr. Rahul Sen ordered.

"Punni! Polish my shoes. I would be going to office in a jiffy." The elder of the two shouted. The arrogant young man in his thirties seemed to be drunk in delight at the prospect of his newly set up business.

"Punni! Where are you? When will you grind the poppyseeds? I am falling short of time. I would have to rush to RumiBoudi's place today. She is throwing a party tonight to celebrate her anniversary." Shouted Romola, the cook, from the kitchen.

Finally, Monideepa, the former chief medical officer of a renowned hospital, ended the instructions with a bang.

"Punni! Your first and foremost job is to come to me and help me pleat my saree. Then you will do the other things." Her commanding voice could shake anyone from top to bottom.

Punni rushed to her. How could she ignore her? She adored her like the Hindu Goddess Parvati who is worshipped for her compassion and motherly love. Monideepa had given her a new life. Punni was left in the hospital ward after her birth. She was only four days old when her mother died. Her father had no soft corner for her as she had failed to acquire the male organ that could offer her at least some sort of security in their patriarchal society. She was treated like an animal by him and was thrown away on the hospital corridor wrapped in a bundle of cloth, near Monideepa's cabin. The nurses found her crying in a feeble voice and brought her to Monideepa. It was years ago when Monideepa engaged one of the nurses to take care of her and brought her home. At that time Rumi, Monideepa's daughter was only three years old and her elder brother, Ratul, who was a haughty naughty five-year -old boy, never felt happy about her intrusion in their lives.

Punni was a version of quiet grace with deep sorrowful eyes holding the weight of unspoken dreams. She grew up into a beautiful young woman and was brilliant as domestic help. She had learnt to read and write from Afzal, the young Muslim compounder,who was stationed at the outhouse of Dr. Rahul Sen. Monideepa named her Punni that means virtue in Bengali. She thought she would be blessed by gods for her good deed and tried to raise her up like her own daughter, but Dr. Rahul Sen had a heart hardened by pragmatism. However, Punni had no regrets. She was like the silent breeze, swift but unnoticed,carrying out her mistress's commands. She would bow her head in quiet deference, like a sunflower turning towards the sun, always seeking approval but never demanding it.

Dr. Rahul Sen and Dr. Monideepa were inseparable. They worked in different hospitals, but used to leave the house together in the morning and came back at lunchtime. Then again they left after an hour. Afzal also had to follow the same routine as he was the right hand of doctor Rahul. A handsome young man of twenty with fair complexion, beautiful eyes and a robust body was a heart-throb of many young nurses, but Afzal had never bothered about them. His steps were light. His presence was softer than a whisper. He was like a shadow that follows, but never leads. Punni, after her afternoon schedules, would visit him with some special recipe stealthily as he used to prepare his lunch by himself. He adored the affectionate glance that Punni bestowed on him.

"Why do you take so much pains for me, Punni?" He would ask timidly.

"Why do you teach me the language and Maths free of cost?" Punni would retort and would smile like a blushing rose.

Her feelings were as delicate as a candle melting away to spread its light without sharing any warmth for herself. Their relationship was silent but eloquent in their attempts to help and heal each other.

Afzal could not be proclaimed as a mighty warrior as his features depicted a calm and friendly spirit, but an incident transformed him into a chivalrous man.

Things were quite smooth as Punni never derelicted from her duty, but Ratul had never accepted her role in the house. He would always try to find some sort of deficiency in her efficiency, yet he could not ignore her beautiful, hypnotic glances and her serene graceful radiance like the morning sun in winter. A quiet sapling she was, slender and unassuming! The sudden advent of youth graced her limbs like the flexible, swaying branches of willow, the innocent eyes radiated a glow from within as if a quiet fire was dormant in her spirit. She blossomed with each passing day like the strokes of a painter, sharpening her features to create a masterpiece.

It was Monideepa's birthday. All the members of the family gathered at the party thrown by Dr. Rahul Sen. The guests included Monideepa's colleagues and Dr. Rahul's business partners as he had started his own nursing home where Ratul also had a significant role to play. After doing his MD, he had joined his father's business and it flourished by leaps and bounds.

The grand banquet hall shimmered with the golden glow of crystal chandeliers. The long wooden table with antique architecture adorned with the finest China was overflowing with delicacies displaying wealth and indulgence. The air buzzed with laughter and excitement. The clinking of crystal goblets filled with the richest wine, added to the charm. A grand three tired cake layered with pink sugared roses and golden balls matched with Monideepa's gorgeous crimson saree. The soft lilting melody created an ambiance of mesmerizing admiration for the birthday girl who, however, was in her late forties. The guests showered her with words of encouragement and inspiration as she was going to retire from her post shortly. The celebration was about to end around midnight. The guests left. Monideepa and Dr.Rahul Sen moved towards their room with satisfaction.

"You look gorgeous! My darling!" said Dr. Rahul.

"Really?" Feigned his wife with her painted lips, perhaps trying to ignore the fact that beauty and power are like the flames of a candle, flickering before they grow dim.

Then they locked their bedroom. Rumi bid goodbye to her boyfriend and her friends and went to her room. Only Ratul had been standing in the balcony with the glass of whiskey. He missed his girlfriend who had left him due to his misbehavior.

Punni tried to clean the hall as she would be busy in the morning. Suddenly the weather changed. Already it was cloudy. The lightning split the sky. Wind howled through the open windows. The door near the balcony burst open.

Afzal helped the caterer to wind up and was about to leave for his room. Suddenly he heard a loud bang and rushed to the hall.

"Leave me Sir! Please leave me! Why are you after me Sir? I am not your cup of tea, Sir! I would shout! Help! Help!"

Afzal rushed to the spot. All the servants except one had left and it was Punni who was struggling like a wounded bird within the arms of Ratul who was trying to kiss her and molest her. The new servant, Ramesh, was staring at them with wide eyes. He couldn't decide whether he should help Punni as he could lose his job.

"What is in your mind, you beautiful bitch? I am your boss and whatever I would like to do, I can do with you." Ratul was murmuring and was trying to unbutton her dress.

"No Sir! You can't !Leave me Sir! Please…"

Afzal could not wait any longer. He went near Ratul and stealthily went behind him so that he could pull him away and release Punni from his clutches. Ratul was completely drunk. He staggered to his feet, his eyes flashing with rage.

"Who are you to interfere, hey bastard! How dare you to challenge me?" Growled Ratul Sen, the apple of his father's eyes.

"Sir !Please leave her. You are committing a crime Sir! Please leave her." Said Afzal.

Ratul threw the glass towards Afzal and rushed at Punni who tried to run away. The glass hit the forehead of Afzal. Blood oozed out and started flowing down his face.

Ratul caught hold of Punni once more, dragging her down.

Afzal took a deep breath and got a rolling pin from the kitchen and hit hard on Ratul's head. Ratul fell down and became unconscious. Afzal took hold of Punni and made her sit on the chair. Ramesh rushed to Monideepa's room and knocked hard.

It was around 3am Monideepa opened the door reluctantly. Her husband was deeply in slumber. She didn't wake him up. Ramesh narrated the whole story and she rushed to the hall.

Afzal was sprinkling water on Ratul's face, and he came to his senses.

"Where am I? What has happened to me?" Ratul fumbled.

"I had no option Sir as you were not in your senses. Let me put some ointment on your head. The wound is not deep. It would heal within a day or two. Let me give you an injection too. It would relieve your pain. Forgive me Sir for what I have done. Very sorry!"Afzal said.

Punni ran to Monideepa and sought refuge in her embrace.

Monideepa did not utter a word. Her glaring eyes could reveal the amount of hatred for her son. Slowly she took Punni towards her attic and asked her to lock the door as from that day Punni was stationed downstairs in the adjacent room where Monideepa used to sleep.

Monideepa was happy that Afzal was really a loyal and righteous man who never thought of losing his job and acted like a hero. Later she fixed a date and Afzal and Punni tied the knot.

Punni and Afzal were shifted to a new location. The new room with a kitchen and washroom was surrounded by the beautiful garden where they started their new journey. Monideepa endowed Punni and Afzal with a new life and recalled Chatrapati Shivaji who never created any discrimination between caste,creed and religion. She was ashamed of her own son who, however, repented for what he had done. After this incident, Ratul transformed himself into a hero who always stood by the people.

Chhatrapati Shivaji Maharaj who Dreamt Swarajya

By Aurobindo Ghosh

The Brave Boy Who Dreamed 'Swarajya'

Long ago, in the mighty forts of Maharashtra, a boy was born who would one day change history! His name was Shivaji, and he was no ordinary child. From the moment he opened his eyes on February 19, 1630, in Shivneri Fort, it was clear that he was destined for greatness. His mother Jijabai, looked at him with pride and whispered,

"You will grow up to protect our land and bring justice to our people!"

A Warrior's Childhood

Unlike other children, Shivaji was drawn to the tales of great warriors and kings. His mother, Jijabai, would tell him about Lord Ram, Arjuna, and the mighty Raja Harishchandra, who stood for truth, bravery, and righteousness. These stories filled young Shivaji's heart with fire. He would often gaze at the majestic forts on the mountains and dream of making them strongholds for a free land.

But dreams were not enough; Shivaji had to be ready to fight for his people. Under the guidance of wise teachers and experienced warriors like Dadoji Kondodev and his mother, he learned:

Sword fighting: he could swing his blade so fast that his enemies wouldn't see it coming!

Horse riding: he could ride through dense forests and rocky hills without stopping!

Archery: his arrows never missed their target!

Even as a child, Shivaji was bold. Once, he saw a group of Mughal soldiers harassing villagers near his home. Without a second thought, he grabbed a stick, led his friends, and chased the soldiers away! The villagers cheered and Shivaji knew this was his calling!

Shivaji's First Victory – The Birth of Swarajya!

By the time he was 15, Shivaji had gathered a small band of brave, loyal warriors. He looked at the mighty forts ruled by unjust rulers and thought, *"Why should someone else control our land? This is our motherland, and we must protect it!"*

What was his first target? It was the mighty Torna Fort! It stood tall on a hill, controlled by the Adil Shahi rulers. But Shivaji had a plan; he and his men climbed the steep hill at night, sneaking past the enemy guards using his numerous pets of monitor lizards, which helped them to climb the steep hill. He suddenly attacked the sleeping bregade of the enemy force and defeated them within no time. As the sun rose, the fort belonged to Shivaji! At just 16 years old, he had conquered his first fort!

One victory led to another; Rajgad, Kondhana (Sinhagad), and Purandar soon fell into Shivaji's hands. The people cheered, calling him their protector. The dream of Swarajya (self-rule) was no longer just a dream; it was becoming real!

The Fearless Leader Who Never Gave Up

Shivaji's enemies were rich and powerful, but he had something they didn't; a heart that beat for his people. He never fought for greed; he fought for justice. With his guerrilla warfare tactics, he struck like lightning and vanished before his enemies could react! He built a mighty navy to protect India's coasts, and in 1674, he was crowned Chhatrapati (King) of the Marathas at Raigad Fort. But even as a great king, Shivaji never forgot his people. He treated women with respect, protected farmers, and believed in religious harmony.

The Rise of the Maratha Empire: A Kingdom of Courage and Freedom

By the time Shivaji turned 15, he was no longer just a warrior; he was a leader. With a heart full of courage and a mind sharper than a sword, he knew that to protect his people, he had to build a kingdom of his own. And so, the story of the Maratha Empire began!

The First Victory: Conquering the Mighty Forts (1645-1656)

As told earlier Shivaji's journey started with Torna Fort in 1645. Climbing its steep walls with a handful of brave men, he captured it in a daring nighttime raid. Soon, he took control of Purandar, Raigad, and Kondana (later renamed Sinhagad), making them strongholds of Swarajya (self-rule).

His enemies laughed at first. *"A young boy is challenging great sultans and emperors? Impossible!"* they thought. But Shivaji's victories soon shook the entire Deccan!

The Battle against the Adil Shahi Sultanate (1656-1660)

The Legend of the Tiger Claws; Shivaji vs. Afzal Khan

Shivaji's rise worried the rulers of Bijapur and the Mughals. They sent their most dangerous general, Afzal Khan, a giant of a man, to defeat him. Afzal Khan had a plan to trick Shivaji into a fake peace meeting and kill him.

Shivaji's advisors warned him, but he was always one step ahead! He wore hidden armor under his clothes and carried a special weapon tiger claws (waghnakh), sharp iron claws hidden in his hand.

When they met, Afzal Khan pretended to hug Shivaji, but suddenly, he pulled out a dagger to stab him! But before he could strike, Shivaji slashed his tiger claws across Afzal Khan's chest! The mighty general fell, and Shivaji's army defeated his forces!

This victory sent shockwaves through the enemy camps: the small Maratha army had crushed a giant! Shivaji was no longer just a warrior; he was a legend!

This victory sent waves of fear through his enemies, and Shivaji's Maratha army grew stronger.

The Mughals vs. Shivaji

A Battle of Wits (1660-1665)

Shivaji's next great enemy was the Mughal Emperor Aurangzeb, the most powerful ruler in India at the time. Furious at Shivaji's growing power, Aurangzeb ordered his general Jai Singh to capture him. After fierce battles, Shivaji was forced to sign the Treaty of Purandar in 1665, surrendering some forts. But he never lost hope. With clever strategies, he regained his power and prepared for his next move.

The Great Escape from Agra (1666)

In 1666, Aurangzeb invited Shivaji to his court in Agra, pretending to honor him. But it was a trap! The moment Shivaji arrived; he was imprisoned in a heavily guarded palace. For months, he was kept under watch. But could a cage hold a lion? Never! Using his brilliant mind, Shivaji pretended to be sick, and soon, large baskets of sweets and fruits were sent into his room daily. One day, he hid inside a giant fruit basket, while his loyal men carried him past the Mughal guards. Before anyone could realize, Shivaji had escaped! He traveled in disguise, moving across India for weeks, until he finally reached Maharashtra, where his people welcomed him as a hero! The plan worked! Shivaji escaped from under the Mughals' noses and returned back, ready to fight for Swarajya again!

The Birth of an Empire; Coronation as Chhatrapati (1674)

After years of battles and victories, Shivaji was ready to rule as a king! On June 6, 1674, in the grand Raigad Fort, he was crowned as Chhatrapati (King) of the Marathas. With golden armor, a royal crown, and thousands of people cheering his name, he declared:

"This land belongs to its people. We will protect it, and we will never bow to injustice!"

Thus, the Maratha Empire was born; an empire built on courage, honor, and freedom!

Chhatrapati Shivaji Maharaj: A Visionary Leader and Master Strategist

Chhatrapati Shivaji Maharaj was not only a fearless warrior but also a brilliant administrator and military strategist. His leadership transformed the Marathas from a scattered group of local warriors into a formidable empire that stood strong against the mightiest forces of the time, including the Mughals, Adil Shahis, Portuguese, British, and Siddis.

Shivaji's Military Strategies: the Art of Asymmetric Warfare

Shivaji Maharaj revolutionized the way wars were fought in India. At a time when the Mughals and Deccan Sultanates relied on large standing armies, heavy artillery, and open-field battles, Shivaji mastered the art of Guerrilla Warfare, which he termed Ganimi Kava (enemy deception tactics).

1. Surprise Attacks and Swift Retreats:

o His forces would attack enemy camps and forts at night or during unfavorable weather, striking quickly and disappearing into the hills and forests.

o This prevented his smaller army from engaging in direct battles with numerically superior forces.

2. Use of Geography:

o The Sahyadri mountain range and dense forests of Maharashtra became his strongest allies.

o He built and captured forts on strategic hilltops, making it extremely difficult for enemy armies to launch attacks.

3. Fort Warfare and Strategic Strongholds:

o Unlike other kings who relied on massive cities, Shivaji focused on building and securing over 300 forts, including Rajgad, Pratapgad, Raigad, and Sinhagad.

o His forts had hidden water sources, granaries, and escape routes, ensuring his army could withstand long sieges.

4. Intelligence and Espionage:

- He created an efficient spy network that gathered crucial information about enemy movements, allowing him to stay one step ahead at all times.

- His spies infiltrated enemy ranks, supplying him with intelligence that often turned the tide of battles.

5. A Powerful and Innovative Navy:

- Realizing the importance of naval dominance, Shivaji built a strong navy, the first of its kind in medieval India.

- His navy, equipped with Maratha warships, cannons, and well-trained sailors, effectively countered the Siddis of Janjira, Portuguese, and British forces along the western coast.

- He constructed coastal forts like Sindhudurg and Vijaydurg, which were impregnable to sea-based attacks.

6. Respect for Local Populations:

- Unlike invading armies that looted and burned villages, Shivaji instructed his soldiers never to harm civilians or temples.

- This made him beloved by the common people, who often supported him and his soldiers with food, shelter, and intelligence.

Shivaji's Administrative Excellence: The Pillars of Swarajya

While Shivaji is celebrated as a military genius, his administration was equally visionary. His governance was based on fairness, efficiency, and inclusivity, ensuring that the Maratha kingdom thrived economically and socially.

1. The Ashtapradhan Mandal – The Eight Pillars of Governance

Shivaji established a council of eight ministers (Ashtapradhan), each responsible for a key area of administration:

1. Peshwa (Prime Minister): Chief advisor to the king and head of the administration.

2. Amatya (Finance Minister): Managed revenue and state treasury.

3. Shurnavis/Sachiv (Secretary): Handled correspondence and records.

4. Mantri (Interior Minister): Kept records of daily activities and espionage reports.

5. Senapati (Commander-in-Chief): Led the military and planned defense strategies.

6. Sumant (Foreign Minister): Handled diplomatic relations with other states and empires.

7. Nyayadhish (Chief Justice): Ensured justice and law enforcement.

8. Panditrao (Religious Affairs Minister): Oversaw religious policies and spiritual matters.

This structured government ensured smooth administration, accountability, and efficiency, making Shivaji's rule one of the best organized in Indian history.

2. Religious Tolerance and Social Welfare

Despite being a staunch Hindu ruler, Shivaji never discriminated against other religions.

Muslims, Christians, and other communities were treated with respect under his rule. Unlike the Mughals and Deccan Sultanates, who imposed the Jizya tax on non-Muslims, Shivaji abolished such unfair taxes. He appointed Muslim officers and soldiers in his army based on merit, not religion. Women were highly respected in his kingdom: his laws strictly punished crimes against women, unlike other rulers who allowed such atrocities.

3. Land Revenue and Economy

Shivaji implemented progressive tax policies to ensure farmers and traders flourished:

Fixed Land Revenue System: Farmers paid taxes based on the fertility of their land, preventing exploitation. Trade and Commerce Protection: Traders and businessmen were given protection from dacoits and corrupt officials, boosting trade. Maritime Trade Expansion: His navy secured trade routes, allowing Indian merchants to conduct business without fear of foreign naval attacks.

Later Years and Expansion (1674-1680)

After his grand coronation in 1674, Shivaji continued expanding his empire:

He led successful campaigns in Karnataka, Vellore, and Jinji, securing valuable territories. His forces raided Mughal strongholds, striking fear even in Aurangzeb's empire. Despite constant battles, he ensured his people prospered, his administration remained strong, and his kingdom flourished.

However, in early 1680, he fell seriously ill, and on April 3, 1680, he breathed his last at Raigad Fort. His death left a great void, but his legacy continued through his son Sambhaji Maharaj, who bravely resisted the Mughals.

Legacy of Chhatrapati Shivaji Maharaj

Chhatrapati Shivaji's dream of Swarajya (self-rule) did not end with him. His Maratha warriors continued to fight, and by the 18th century, the Marathas had become the dominant power in India under the Peshwas. With the alliance with Jhanshi ki Rani Laxmibai, Peshwas fought against Britishers. Inspired Freedom Fighters: His spirit of independence inspired leaders like Mahatma Gandhi, Bal Gangadhar Tilak, and Netaji Subhas Chandra Bose. Military genius recognized him worldwide: Even British officers studied his guerrilla tactics for modern warfare. Chhatrapati is a National Hero: Statues, forts, and historical sites in his honor stand as symbols of courage and self-respect.

Chhatrapati Shivaji Maharaj was more than just a warrior; he was a visionary leader, a champion of justice, and an architect of modern governance. His ability to defy the mighty Mughals and European colonial powers proves that bravery, intelligence, and determination can overcome any challenge. Even today, the slogan used by Chhatrapati followers is Jai Bhavani! Jai Shivaji!

Shivaji, the Maratha Legend

By Devajit Bhuyan

Shivaji, the legendary Maratha general and king was born on 19 February 1630 in the fort of Shinveri, present day Pune of Maharashtra. His paternal grandfather Maloji was from the Bhonsle clan and was an influential general of Ahmednagar Sultanate. Maloji was awarded the title Raja (king) by the Sultanate and rights over Pune and some nearby areas to provide for military service and for his expenses. Maloji was also given the fort of Shinveri for his residence and keeping his army.

At the time of the birth of Shivaji, the power of the south India and western India was shared by Islamic Sultanate of Bijapur, Ahmednagar, Golkonda and the Mughal Emperor. Shivaji's father Sahaji joined the service of Bijapur and obtained Poona (now Pune) as grant. Later, Sahaji was posted at Bangalore by the Bijapur ruler Adilshah and appointed Dadoji as Poona's administrator. After death of Dadoji, without any appointment by Bijapur ruler or taking the consent of the Sultan, Shivaji took control of Poona and directly challenged the ruler of Bijapur.

During those days changing allegiance by kings because of bribery and money was common like political leaders of today changing sides for money, power and position. At the age of 16 years in the year 1646, Shivaji captured Torna Fort bribing the officials of the fort taking confusion of the situation of serious illness of Bijapur sultan Adil Shah. Shivaji seized a huge quantity of treasures from the fort of Torna to consolidate his military and political power. With his resources gained from Torna Fort treasury, Shivaji build a new fort Rajgarh and took direct control of Baramati, Indapur and Kalyan. Later, differences arose between Sahaji and his son Shivaji regarding relationships with nearby other rulers under Bijapur Sultanate and control of Bijapur over Maratha areas. Sahaji told Bijapur Sultanate to take any action they wished to take against rebellious approach of his son Shivaji.

The Bijapur Sultanate was displeased with their losses to Shivaji's forces, with their vassal Shahaji disavowing his son's actions. After a peace treaty with the Mughals, and the general acceptance of the young Ali Adil Shah II as the sultan, the Bijapur government became more stable and turned its attention towards Shivaji. In 1657, the sultan sent Afzal Khan, a veteran general, to arrest Shivaji. Before engaging him, the Bijapuri forces desecrated the Tulja Bhavani Temple, a holy site for Shivaji's family, and the Vithoba temple at Pandharpur, a major pilgrimage site for Hindus. This has angered Shivaji and Hindu population, and they vowed to fight with the invaders. Pursued by Bijapuri forces, Shivaji retreated to Pratapgad fort, where many of his colleagues pressed him to surrender. The two forces found themselves at a stalemate, with Shivaji unable to break the siege by Afzal Khan. Though Afzal Khan had a powerful cavalry but lacking siege equipment, was unable to take the fort from determined Shivaji. After two months, Afzal Khan sent an envoy to Shivaji suggesting the two leaders meet in private, outside the fort, for negotiations. The two met in a hut in the foothills of Pratapgad fort on 10 November 1659. The arrangements had dictated that each come armed only with a sword and attended by one follower. Shivaji, suspecting Afzal Khan's hidden agenda to arrest or attack him, wore armour beneath his clothes, concealed a bagh nakh ("tiger claw") on his left arm, and had a dagger in his right hand. As both could not come to an agreement, the two-warrior started to fight and wound up in a physical struggle that proved fatal for Khan. Shivaji then with his hidden troops attacked the Bijapuri army. In the ensuing Battle of Pratapgarh, Shivaji's forces decisively defeated the Bijapur Sultanate's forces. However showing his greatness, Shivaji set free all the enemy soldiers, officers and sent back to their homes with money, food, and other gifts.

After defeat of the forces of Afzal Khan, the Bijapuri forces were sent again to capture Shivaji. Shivaji and his army marched towards the Konkan coast and Kolhapur, seizing Panhala fort, and defeating Bijapuri forces sent against them, under Rustam Zaman and Fazl Khan, in 1659. In 1660, Adilshah sent his general Siddi Jauhar to attack Shivaji's southern border, in alliance with the Mughals who planned to attack from the north. At that time, Shivaji was encamped at Panhala fort with his forces. Siddi Jauhar's army besieged Panhala in mid-1660, cutting off supply routes to the fort. During the bombardment of Panhala, Siddi Jauhar purchased grenades from the English at Rajapur and also hired some English artillerymen to assist in his bombardment of the fort, conspicuously flying a flag used by the English. This perceived betrayal angered Shivaji, who in December retaliated by plundering the English factory at Rajapur and capturing four of the owners, imprisoning them until mid-1663. After months of siege, Shivaji negotiated with Siddi Jauhar and handed over the fort on 22 September 1660, withdrawing to Vishalgad. In the battle of Pavan Khind Shivaji escaped from Panhala by cover of night, and as he was pursued by the enemy cavalry, his Maratha sardar Baji Prabhu Deshpande of Bandal Deshmukh, along with 300 soldiers, volunteered to fight to the death to hold back the enemy at Ghod Khind ("horse ravine") to give Shivaji and the rest of the army a chance to reach the safety of the Vishalgad fort.

Until 1657, Shivaji maintained peaceful relations with the Mughal Empire. Shivaji offered his assistance to Aurangzeb, the son of the Mughal Emperor and viceroy of the Deccan, in conquering Bijapur, in return for formal recognition of his right to the Bijapuri forts and villages in his possession. Dissatisfied with the Mughal response, and receiving a better offer from Bijapur, he launched a raid into the Mughal Deccan. Shivaji's confrontations with the Mughals began in March 1657, when two of Shivaji's officers raided the Mughal territory near Ahmednagar. This was followed by raids in Junnar and Aurangzeb responded to the raids by sending Nasiri Khan, who defeated the forces of Shivaji at Ahmednagar. However, Aurangzeb's countermeasures against Shivaji were interrupted by the rainy season and his battles with his brothers over the succession to the Mughal throne, following the illness of the emperor Shah Jahan.

Chhatrapati - The Legacy!

At the request of Bijapur Sulnate, Aurangzeb, after becoming the Mughal emperor, sent his maternal uncle Shaista Khan, with big army. In January 1660 to attack Shivaji in conjunction with Bijapur's army led by Siddi Jauhar. Shaista Khan, with his better equipped and well provisioned army seized Pune. He also took the nearby fort of Chakan. Shaista Khan established his residence at Shivaji's palace of Lal Mahal. On the night of 5 April 1663, Shivaji led a daring night attack on Shaista Khan's camp. He, along with 400 men, attacked Shaista Khan's mansion, broke into Khan's bedroom and wounded him. Khan lost three fingers. In the scuffle, Shaista Khan's son and several wives, servants, and soldiers were killed. The Khan took refuge with the Mughal forces outside of Pune, and Aurangzeb punished him for this embarrassment with a transfer to Bengal. In retaliation for Shaista Khan's attacks, and to replenish his now-depleted treasury, in 1664 Shivaji sacked the port city of Surat, a wealthy Mughal trading centre. On 13 February 1665, he also conducted a naval raid on Portuguese-held Basrur in present-day Karnataka.

The attacks on Shaista Khan and Surat enraged Aurangzeb. In response, he sent the Rajput general Jai Singh I with an army to defeat Shivaji. Throughout 1665, Jai Singh's forces pressed Shivaji, with their cavalry razing the countryside, and besieging Shivaji's forts. The Mughal commander succeeded in luring away several of Shivaji's key commanders, and many of his cavalrymen, into Mughal service. By mid-1665, with the fortress at Purandar besieged and near capture, Shivaji was forced to come to terms with Jai Singh. In the Treaty of Purandar, signed by Shivaji and Jai Singh on 11 June 1665, Shivaji agreed to give up 23 of his forts, keeping 12 for himself, and pay compensation to the Mughals. Shivaji agreed to become a vassal of the Mughal empire, and to send his son Sambhaji, along with 5,000 horsemen, to fight for the Mughals in the Deccan.

In 1666, Aurangzeb summoned Shivaji to Agra, along with his nine-year-old son Sambhaji. Aurangzeb planned to send Shivaji to Kandahar, now in Afghanistan, to consolidate the Mughal empire's northwestern frontier. However, on 12 May 1666, Shivaji was made to stand at court alongside relatively low-ranking nobles, men he had already defeated in battle. Shivaji's ego and self-esteem was hurt, and he thought it as an insult and stormed out. Soon Shivaji was placed under house arrest. Ram Singh, son of Jai Singh, guaranteed custody of Shivaji and his son. Shivaji's position under house arrest was perilous, as Aurangzeb's court debated whether to kill him or continue to employ him. Jai Singh, having assured Shivaji of his personal safety, tried to influence Aurangzeb's decision. Meanwhile, Shivaji hatched a plan to free himself. He sent most of his men back home and asked Ram Singh to withdraw his guarantees to the emperor for the safe custody of himself and his son. He surrendered to Mughal forces. Shivaji then pretended to be ill and began sending out large baskets packed with sweets to be given to the Brahmins and poor as penance. One day, by putting himself in one of the baskets and his son Sambhaji in another, Shivaji escaped and left Agra. After his escape, peace talks with the Mughals started again with the Mughal sardar Jaswant Singh acting as an intermediary between Shivaji and Aurangzeb for new peace proposals. Between 1666 and 1668, Aurangzeb conferred the title of raja on Shivaji. Sambhaji was also restored as a Mughal mansabdar with 5,000 horses. Shivaji at that time sent Sambhaji, with general Prataprao Gujar, to serve with the Mughal viceroy in Aurangabad. Aurangzeb also permitted Shivaji to attack Bijapur, ruled by the decaying Adil Shahi dynasty; the weakened Sultan Ali Adil Shah II sued for peace and granted the rights of sardeshmukhi and chauthai to Shivaji.

The peace between Shivaji and the Mughals lasted until 1670, after which Aurangzeb became suspicious of the close ties between Shivaji and Mu'azzam, who he thought might usurp his throne, and may even have been receiving bribes from Shivaji. Also at that time, Aurangzeb, occupied in fighting the Afghans, greatly reduced his army in the Deccan; many of the disbanded soldiers quickly joined Maratha service. The Mughals also took away the jagir of Berar from Shivaji to recover the money lent to him a few years earlier. In response, Shivaji launched an offensive against the Mughals and in a span of four months recovered a major portion of the territories that had been surrendered to them. Shivaji sacked Surat for a second time in 1670; the English and Dutch factories were able to repel his attack, but he managed to sack the city itself. Angered by the renewed attacks, the Mughals resumed hostilities with the Marathas, sending a force under Daud Khan to intercept Shivaji on his return home from Surat; this force was defeated in the Battle of Vani-Dindori near present-day Nashik. In October 1670, Shivaji sent his forces to harass the English at Bombay; as they had refused to sell him war materiel, his forces blocked English woodcutting parties from leaving Bombay. In September 1671, Shivaji sent an ambassador to Bombay, again seeking materiel, this time for the fight against Danda-Rajpuri. The English had misgivings of the advantages Shivaji would gain from this conquest, but also did not want to lose any chance of receiving compensation for his looting their factories at Rajapur. The English sent Lieutenant Stephen Ustick to treat with Shivaji, but negotiations failed over the issue of the Rajapur indemnity. Numerous exchanges of envoys followed over the coming years, with some agreement as to the arms issues in 1674, but Shivaji was never to pay the Rajapur indemnity before his death, and the factory there dissolved at the end of 1682.

Shivaji had acquired extensive lands and wealth through his campaigns, but lacking a formal title, he was still technically a Mughal zamindar or the son of a Bijapuri jagirdar, with no legal basis to rule his de facto domain. A kingly title could address this and also prevent any challenges by other Maratha leaders, who were his equals. Such a title would also provide the Hindu Marathis with a fellow Hindu sovereign in a region otherwise ruled by Muslims. The preparation for a proposed coronation began in 1673. On 6 June 1674, Shivaji was crowned king of the Maratha Empire (Hindavi Swaraj) in a lavish ceremony at Raigad fort. In the Hindu calendar it was the 13th day (trayodashi) of the first fortnight of the month of Jyeshtha in the year 1596. Shivaji became entitled to Shakakarta ("founder of an era") and Chhatrapati ("Lord of the Umbrella"). He also took the title of Haindava Dharmodhhaarak (protector of the Hindu faith) and Kshatriya Kulavantas: Kshatriya being the varna of Hinduism and kulavantas meaning the 'head of the kula, or clan'.

Beginning in 1674, the Marathas undertook an aggressive campaign, raiding Khandesh, capturing Bijapuri Ponda, Karwar, and Kolhapur. In November, the Maratha navy skirmished with the Siddis of Janjira, but failed to dislodge them. Having recovered from an illness, and taking advantage of a civil war that had broken out between the Deccanis and the Afghans at Bijapur, Shivaji raided Athani in 1676. In the run-up to his expedition, Shivaji appealed to a sense of Deccani patriotism, that Southern India was a homeland that should be protected from outsiders. His appeal was somewhat successful, and in 1677 Shivaji visited Hyderabad for a month and entered into a treaty with the Qutubshah of the Golkonda sultanate, who agreed to renounce his alliance with Bijapur and jointly oppose the Mughals. In 1677, Shivaji invaded Karnataka with 30,000 cavalry and 40,000 infantry, backed by Golkonda artillery and funding. Proceeding south, Shivaji seized the forts of Vellore and Gingee; the latter served as a capital of the Marathas during the reign of his son Rajaram I.

Shivaji maintained a small but effective standing army. The core of Shivaji's army consisted of peasants of Maratha and Kunbi castes. Shivaji was aware of the limitations of his army. He realised that conventional warfare methods were inadequate to confront the big, well-trained cavalry of the Mughals, which was equipped with field artillery. As a result, Shivaji mastered guerilla tactics which became known as Ganimi Kawa in the Marathi language. His strategies consistently perplexed and defeated armies sent against him. He realized that the most vulnerable point of the large, slow-moving armies of the time was supply. He utilised knowledge of the local terrain and the superior mobility of his light cavalry to cut off supplies to the enemy. Shivaji refused to confront the enemy in pitched battles. Instead, he lured the enemies into difficult hills and jungles of his own choosing, catching them at a disadvantage and routing them. Shivaji did not adhere to a particular tactic but used several methods to undermine his enemies, as required by circumstances, such as sudden raids, sweeps and ambushes, and psychological warfare. Aware of the need for naval power to maintain control along the Konkan coast, Shivaji began to build his navy in 1657 or 1659, with the purchase of twenty galivants from the Portuguese shipyards of Bassein. With the Marathas being accustomed to a land-based military, Shivaji widened his search for qualified crews for his ships, taking on lower-caste Hindus of the coast who were long familiar with naval operations (the famed "Malabar pirates"), as well as Muslim mercenaries. Noting the power of the Portuguese navy, Shivaji hired a number of Portuguese sailors and Goan Christian converts, and made Rui Leitao Viegas commander of his fleet. Viegas was later to defect back to the Portuguese, taking 300 sailors with him. Shivaji fortified his coastline by seizing coastal forts and refurbishing them. He built his first marine fort at Sindhudurg, which was to become the headquarters of the Maratha navy.

Shivaji was considered to be a regional hero till 19th century, when Jyotirao Phule put him before the Indian people who fought the Mughals for sovereignty of his mother land and safeguard Hinduism. Slowly with her writings other authors are also inspired to put Shivaji as a national Hindu hero to motivate people for independence of India. However, one section of historians hides the truth that Shivaji was also an army general under Muslim rulers and projected Shivaji as a Hindu hero who fought with Muslim rulers and saved Hindu population and Hinduism from the expansionist Islam and clutches of Aurangzeb who was an orthodox Muslim and tried to convert Hindu kings and people by hook or by crook. Shivaji knew it well that the divided small Hindu kings were not capable to fight the mighty Mughal Emperor Aurangzeb and so used all tricks and politics for the survival and expansion of his kingdom. Sometimes he sided with Bijapur and sometimes with other kingdoms for his territory. It is said that everything is fair in love and war. Shivaji was aware of this and expert in luring his enemies and adversaries and defeat them in opportune moment. His war skills were superior in comparison to other Hindu kings of that time and so Aurangzeb tried to keep Shivaji in good humour. But rebellious minded Shivaji from young age always followed his own path and most of the time refused to succumb to pressure from others.

If a comparative study is done between Shivaji and contemporary Ahom General Lachit Barphukan, who defeated the Mughal army of Aurangzeb, it is observed that Shivaji compromised with the Mughals Emperor Aurangzeb several times and even fought battle in favour of the Mughals. Shivaji was not a sovereign king with definite territory of kingdom whereas the Ahom were sovereign king with many subordinate kings playing tribute to them. To become blow hot-blow cold was master strategy to engage with mighty Mughals. Shivaji became hostile to the Mughal Emperor after he was not given due respect in the Mughal Darbar (parliament) and subsequently kept under house arrest. Lachit Barphukan refused to compromise with the Mughal Emperor Aurangzeb and his General Ram Singha at any cost and instead fought the Mughals tooth and nail to defeat them.

For Lachit integrity and sovereignty of the Ahom Kingdom was prime factor. Whereas Shivaji flip-flopped with the Mughals depending upon situations, convenience and compromised with sovereignty. Though Shivaji was a great Hindu warrior of the time of Mughals, early historians considered him as a Robinhood type of legendary warrior. Contrary to this Lachit Barphukan was a great General and warrior defending Ahom kingdom from the combined strength of Muslim and Hindu warlords of Mughal Empire and convincingly defeating them. Lachit Barphukan fought with Mughal Emperor killing his own uncle and leading naval forces from sick bed for the nation of Assam, Assamese nationality going above religions. For Shivaji survival was the basic instinct for fighting the mighty Mughals and his flip-flop approach was part of his war strategy. Reality is that both Shivaji and Lachit Barphukan were instrumental for safeguarding the Hindu culture and religions from the clutches of hostile, aggressive Mughal kings and their generals.

(N.B. The years and dates are taken from open sources of history, and the author cannot confirm authenticity of the dates and years given in the writeup)

A Dream That Came True

By Priyadarshi Ravi

Synopsis

"A Dream That Came True" is a powerful historical narration that brings to life the extraordinary journey of Chhatrapati Shivaji Maharaj—a visionary leader who dared to dream of a unified and independent land free from oppression. The prose explores how Shivaji, against all odds, transformed his vision of Swarajya (self-rule) into a reality, not just through military conquests but through strategic governance, diplomacy, and an unwavering belief in justice.

The story takes readers through his early inspirations, battles, alliances, and revolutionary administrative policies, showcasing how his dream was not just about territorial expansion but about empowering people. It highlights Shivaji's foresight in fortification, naval strength, and governance, making him a ruler far ahead of his time.

His dream was not just his own—it became a beacon of hope for future generations. The prose also explores how his ideals of unity, self-reliance, and resistance against oppression continued to inspire India's freedom struggle, proving that a dream backed by vision and action can indeed come true.

A Dream That Came True

History has witnessed the rise and fall of many rulers, but only a few leave behind a legacy that shapes the destiny of a nation. Chhatrapati Shivaji Maharaj was one such leader whose vision was not just to establish a kingdom but to unite a fragmented land under one strong and just rule. His dream was to create a Swarajya, a self-rule where his people could live with dignity, free from oppression and foreign dominance. This dream, which once seemed impossible, became a reality through his courage, intelligence, and relentless efforts.

The Birth of a Visionary

Shivaji was born in 1630 at Shivneri Fort to Shahaji Bhonsle and Jijabai. From an early age, he was exposed to tales of bravery and justice, shaping his vision of an independent kingdom. His mother, Jijabai, played a crucial role in instilling the values of righteousness and patriotism in him. She often narrated stories of Ramayana and Mahabharata, inspiring him to stand against injustice.

At a time when the Indian subcontinent was divided among various rulers, including the Mughals, Adil Shahi Sultanate, and Portuguese, the idea of a unified and independent land seemed like a distant dream. But Shivaji was not one to accept the status quo. He saw the pain of his people, the tyranny of foreign rulers, and the oppression faced by local communities. This ignited in him a desire to change the course of history.

A Leader is Born

Shivaji's leadership skills became evident at a young age. At just 15, he began capturing forts and laying the foundation of what would later become the great Maratha Empire. His first conquest, the Torna Fort, was symbolic—it was not just a military victory but a declaration of his intent to reclaim the land for its rightful heirs. This marked the beginning of his lifelong mission.

Unlike other rulers who relied solely on brute force, Shivaji was a master strategist. He understood that diplomacy and alliances were as important as military strength. He built a network of trusted generals, advisers, and spies who helped him execute his vision efficiently. He treated his soldiers with respect and ensured they were well taken care of, which earned him immense loyalty.

Building an Empire Brick by Brick

Shivaji's dream of a unified and independent land took shape with every fort he captured and every enemy he defeated. He was not reckless in battle; he carefully planned each move, using guerrilla warfare tactics that allowed his smaller forces to defeat mighty armies. His military campaigns were not about expanding power but about securing a free and just rule for his people.

One of his greatest strengths was his ability to turn enemies into allies. He maintained friendly relations with several regional rulers and even negotiated with the Mughals when needed. His diplomatic skills were as sharp as his sword. Even when faced with seemingly insurmountable challenges, he never lost sight of his dream.

His ability to adapt was evident in his naval strategy. Unlike other Indian rulers who focused only on land battles, Shivaji understood the importance of controlling the seas. He built a powerful navy that could counter European threats along the western coast. This was revolutionary for Indian warfare and ensured that his empire remained safe from foreign invasions.

The Icon of Swarajya

Shivaji's dream of Swarajya—self-rule—was realized when he was crowned Chhatrapati in 1674 at Raigad Fort. This coronation was not just a ceremony; it was a statement to the world that India could stand strong and independent. It was proof that his vision was not just a fantasy but a reality that had taken form through determination, sacrifice, and wisdom.

His rule was marked by justice, inclusivity, and a strong administrative system. He introduced policies that favored farmers, promoted trade, and ensured that no community faced discrimination. Unlike many rulers of his time, he respected all religions and upheld the values of tolerance and harmony. His governance set a precedent for future leaders, proving that a ruler's greatness lies not in the size of his kingdom but in the well-being of his people.

Challenges

Despite his successes, Shivaji faced immense challenges. The Mughals, under Aurangzeb, saw him as a major threat. He was once captured and taken to Agra, where Aurangzeb intended to keep him imprisoned for life. But Shivaji's intelligence and courage shone through—he devised a brilliant escape plan, using disguise and deception to flee from the Mughal court. This daring escape became legendary and reinforced his reputation as an invincible leader.

Many tried to crush his dream, but Shivaji never wavered. Every setback only strengthened his resolve. His ability to learn from failures and turn them into victories was what set him apart.

A Legacy That Lives On

Shivaji's dream did not end with his reign. His vision continued to inspire generations of warriors, revolutionaries, and freedom fighters. The Maratha Empire he built stood strong even after his passing, challenging the mighty Mughal rule and influencing the course of Indian history.

Centuries later, leaders like Mahatma Gandhi, Bal Gangadhar Tilak, and Subhas Chandra Bose drew inspiration from Shivaji's life. His spirit of resistance and self-rule fueled India's struggle for independence. Even today, his ideals of bravery, justice, and patriotism resonate deeply in the hearts of millions.

Conclusion: A Dream Fulfilled, A Vision Eternal

Chhatrapati Shivaji Maharaj was not just a king; he was a visionary whose dream of Swarajya reshaped India's destiny. He proved that courage, intelligence, and unwavering determination could turn even the most impossible dreams into reality. His legacy is not just a chapter in history—it is a beacon of hope and inspiration for those who dare to dream of a better tomorrow.

Even today, the echoes of his dream can be heard in the forts he built, the stories of valor he left behind, and the spirit of self-rule that continues to guide India. Chhatrapati Shivaji Maharaj's journey was not just his own—it was the journey of a nation awakening to its strength, a dream that came true not just for him, but for generations to come.

***

The Living Legacy

By Dr Priyanka Joshi

"In the land of Karnataka, amidst the rugged terrains of Gadag province, stood the small yet resilient fort of Belwadi. It was the year 1678 when Chhatrapati Shivaji Maharaj, after a triumphant conquest in the South, marched towards Maharashtra. Along his path, he laid siege to Belwadi, a stronghold that would soon become the stage for an extraordinary tale of courage and honor.

Within the fort resided a fearless warrior—Mallabai Desai. Widowed yet unwavering, she refused to surrender to fate. When the Marathi forces advanced, she stood firm, leading an army of valiant women into battle. Their swords clashed, their spirits soared, and against all odds, they fought with unmatched bravery. The battlefield echoed with the roars of their defiance, and though outnumbered, they stood undeterred.

Chhatrapati Shivaji Maharaj, a ruler who recognized true valour, was deeply moved by Mallabai's courage. Instead of seizing her land, he honored her sacrifice. "For the milk of your children," he declared, "Your kingdom shall be returned to you." His words were not just a gesture of mercy but a tribute to a warrior who fought for her freedom.

But Mallabai's tribute to the great king would be even more enduring. To ensure that Shivaji Maharaj's memory lived on forever, she commissioned the first-ever sculpture of the legendary ruler during his lifetime. The statue, a symbol of admiration and gratitude, found its place in a temple in Yadwad village near Dharwad. It remains the only known contemporary sculpture of the great Chhatrapati, standing as a silent witness to a time of valor, sacrifice, and unwavering honor.

Thus, the tale of Mallabai Desai lives on—not just as a chapter in history, but as a testament to the indomitable spirit of those who choose to fight, no matter the odds."[1]

'How many of you knew this story?' I asked looking at the students. All I could see was clueless eyes gazing back at me.

'None, I suppose...' I paused, not breaking my eye contact with my 48 students who had showed up for class that day. I continued with my lesson.

Losing track of time, I kept talking about the valour of the great Maratha king until the bell rang. I picked up my belongings and walked out of the hall. As I was on my way towards the stairs, a voice called out from behind, "Apeksha ma'am." I turned around to look—it was Harish, a student of mine. Since he was walking towards me, I stopped for him.

'Ma'am, I just wanted to invite you to our programme. We, the students, have organized a celebration on the occasion of Shiv Jayanti (Chhatrapati Shivaji Maharaj's birth anniversary) and I wanted to invite you to

---

[1] *The tale of Mallabai Desai.*

it. We would really like if you could come for it, especially as you are our History teacher.'

'What time?' I asked.

'Next Tuesday at 11am ma'am.'

I was aware the occasion was on the coming Tuesday.

'Surely, I'll come for it.' I smiled. He smiled back.

'Thank you ma'am.' I nodded and turned around to leave.

I am, Apeksha Bhave, a History teacher at a college from Pune in Maharashtra. It is no surprise, that I have not only heard tales of gantry but also seen living evidence of the greatness of the Maratha warriors and one in specific, Chhatrapati Shivaji Maharaj.

As the days passed I saw the students around the college premises, including Harish, preparing for the day excitedly. Their excitement made me look forward to the event even more. Finally, Tuesday arrived. As I entered the college auditorium, there were beautifully designed posters of Chhatrapati Shivaji Maharaj, adorned with quotes highlighting his wisdom and bravery. The students had put in immense effort, which was evident in every detail. The event began with a traditional lamp-lighting ceremony. Harish and a few other students had dressed up in traditional Marathi attire, complete with turbans. They performed a captivating enactment of Chhatrapati Shivaji Maharaj's daring escape from Agra, a tale that never failed to inspire. The audience was mesmerized, and I found myself engrossed in their performance. Next, there were Powada recitations. After an hour of enthusiastic performances, Harish walked to the mic, stepped forward, and began to give the vote of thanks. Amidst it, before he was to invite the honorable Principal of the institute to say a few words, he said, "Now, we request our history teacher, Apeksha ma'am, to share a few words with us."

Although completely expected, I couldn't refuse. I walked up to the stage and took a deep breath while smiling at the eager faces before me.

"Chhatrapati Shivaji Maharaj," I began, "was not just a warrior. He was a visionary, a leader, and an embodiment of resilience. His greatness lay not just in the battles he fought but in the ideals he upheld. He believed in *Swarajya* – self-rule – and justice for all, irrespective of religion or caste."

I could see the students listening intently, their eyes shining with admiration. What can I say about Maharaj that has not already been said earlier?

"Even today, centuries later, his principles remain relevant. If we imbibe even a fraction of his courage, determination, and wisdom in our lives, we can bring about positive change. Remember, history is not just about the past; it is a guide for the future."

There was a moment of silence before the hall echoed in applause. As I stepped down, Harish with a few students came up to me.

'Ma'am, that was inspiring,' Harish said, his voice full of admiration.

I smiled. 'I only spoke what I felt like. But tell me, what inspired you all?'

Harish looked at his friends before answering. 'We felt that in today's times, people are forgetting the true essence of Chhatrapati Shivaji Maharaj's teachings. We wanted to remind everyone, especially our generation, of the greatness of our history.'

His words filled me with pride. 'You have done an excellent job. Chhatrapati Shivaji Maharaj would have been proud to see young minds like yours keeping his legacy alive.'

The event concluded with a rousing rendition of '*Jai Bhavani, Jai Shivaji*!' The energy in the room was electric, and I knew that this celebration would remain in our hearts for a long time. As I walked out of the hall, I couldn't help but feel hopeful. With students like Harish and his friends, the future was in safe hands. The ideals of Shivaji Maharaj would continue to inspire generations to come.

***

Chhatrapati-The Legacy

By Rohan Narvekar

Introduction

Chhatrapati Shivaji Maharaj is hardly a stranger to anyone. Almost everyone has heard his name and stories about his life and achievements. People, especially in Maharashtra, have grown up hearing tales of his bravery & shrewdness. He has been held as a gold standard for how a ruler should be long after his time. Stickers of him and his royal seal adorn numerous vehicles, doors and T-shirts. His potrait can be found hanging on the walls of homes and offices. But do we try to know more? Are we curious about the reason for his enduring legacy and the love we have for him? Let's us try to understand all this from some incidents of his life and the relevance it holds in the present times.

Chapter 1:
Great Things have Small Beginnings

Born on 19th of February 1630 at Shivneri Fort near Junnar in Pune district, Shivaji was the son of Shahaji Bhonsale & Jijabai Bhonsale née Jadhav. The very basic difference between Shivaji and his contemporaries was that Shivaji wasn't born into royalty and didn't inherit a kingdom. All he inherited was a small fief *(Jagir)* from his father Shahaji who was in service of the Bijapuri Sultanate. He was raised by his mother Rajmata Jijabai & educated by Dadoji Kondadev. The fact that Shivaji Maharaj successfully carved out his kingdom from the Southern Sultanates, sets his journey apart from most of his contemporaries.

Shivaji Maharaj could have lived comfortably from the revenue of his *Jagir* or going into the service of the Mughals. But he chose to carve out his own kingdom and create Swaraj. This Swaraj, and the idea of it, would later form the genesis of the Maratha Empire.

★Takeaways: It is not necessary to have immense resources or manpower. Judicious use of available resources coupled with shrewd politics and astute diplomacy can turn the tide in your favour. Even the biggest tree starts out as a small seed. Shivaji Maharaj's life is the very embodiment of it.

Chapter 2:
The Best Start is an Early Start

Shivaji Maharaj was very young when he came to Pune and got involved in the local administrative process. Blessed with Jaijabai & Dadoji Kondadev as his teachers, Maharaj himself must have shown much aptitude and willingness at that age. Not for nothing did he capture his first fort at sixteen years of age. Torna fort is the highest hill- fort in Pune district and very hard to capture. It is said that Shivaji Maharaj used a combination of strategy & bribery to capture the fort. There was confusion in the Bijapuri court owing to the illness of Sultan Mohammad Adil Shah. Taking advantage of this fact, Maharaj used his comrades Tanaji Malusare, Yesaji Kank & Baji Pasalkar as 'influence agents' to bribe the fort-keeper. He kept his men hidden in the woods surrounding the fort. When the Adilshahi army moved towards the fort, Shivaji and his men surprised them with a guerrilla raid and routed them. Some accounts say that the fort was captured without any bloodshed. This is seen in many of his later conquests.

★Takeaways: Shivaji Maharaj started his career at a very early age. We should interpret this as striving towards our goal as and when we find our calling without delay.

The second point is situational awareness in using tactics, when to use diplomacy and when to use force.

What we can take from it is the awareness of where and when to take action and also why to take action.

Chapter 3:
The Cause Behind The Effect

What specific factors make Shivaji Maharaj, such a celebrated figure even though the monarchial system of government has been replaced by democracy in modern times? The simple answer is that Shivaji Maharaj was way ahead of his time. This can be gauged from his views on various aspects of nation building. Many of these factors are intermingled and should been seen as such.

Chapter 4
Agriculture, Revenue System, & A Rotational Army

Before Shivaji came to power, the state of agriculture and revenue was limited to the farmers and the village headmen and therefore, unorganized. The headmen squeezed the villages for maximum tax and never cared about their problems. After Shivaji Maharaj came to power, he realised the importance of agriculture & fair revenue collection for nation building. He ordered proper land measurements done and fixed the revenue rate. Whatever yield the farmer managed to get was divided into five parts. Three parts were for the farmer and two parts taken as revenue. Farmers were empowered and encouraged by providing seeds and cattle. The tax was waived off in times of crisis to be returned in installments later. Soldiers were strictly warned not to harm the crops or ride through them. "Not even the stem of a single vegetable should be touched", were the instructions from Shivaji to his soldiers.

Shivaji Maharaj realised the pitfalls in having a paid mercenary army. Even a full time army was not feasible. He turned to the people itself as a solution. He trained the farmers in combat and created a rotational system where soldering & farming were done alternately in shifts. The soldiers were paid salaries. Such men never destroyed crops as they were reminded of their own farms. They never molested or raped the peasants' women as they were reminded of the women in their own families.

★Takeaways: By creating such a system, Shivaji Maharaj used Social Welfare as a tool to check corruption & barbaric tendencies. His army was meant to prevent the tendency to loot and destroy.

Chapter 5:
Views on Women

Before Shivaji's time, women were barely treated as humans and that's putting it lightly. Rape and probably sexual exploitation were rampant around the land and there was no recourse as the oppressors the very people responsible to mete out justice. Shivaji Maharaj changed all that. His soldiers and officers were expressly forbidden from harming women and children, even those of the enemy. No soldier was to take women with them for gratification or entertainment and that no women should be made a *Batkin* (sort of a sex slave). He even backed his words with actions. How severely he dealt with the Patil (Headman) of Ranjha and his victorious commander Sakuji Gaikwad is widely known. The incident with the daughter-in-law of the *Subhedar* of Kalyan is testament to Shivaji's strength of character and his virtuous view of beauty.

★Takeaways: We can at least learn to be considerate of a woman's modesty and not look the other way when it is being outraged.

Chapter 6:
Religion, Caste, Administration

These aspects truly set Shivaji Maharaj apart from the prevalent social norms and highlights his being ahead of his time. Shivaji never discriminated on the basis of caste and religion. He probably believed in syncretism. Although a devout Hindu, Shivaji was tolerant of different religions. He never tried to assert Hindu beliefs on people of other religions. Hindus and Muslims weren't treated differently during his rule. His soldiers were instructed not to desecrate mosques during expeditions. If they chanced upon the Holy Quran, they were to respectfully hand it over to any Muslims they could find. No Muslim or Hindu women were to be harmed in the any way. Shivaji took them in and acted as their guardian till their relatives could come for them. He even wrote a letter to Aurangzeb urging him to abolish the *Jizya* tax (Religious tax) and behave more like his great grandfather, Emperor Akbar. And so it was with caste.

Shivaji Maharaj employed people of all castes and religions including Muslims in his administration & armed forces. He even employed Europeans. An entry in the *Sabhasad Bakhar* states that people from *Berad, Ramoshi, Aadkari* and other such communities were given employment. The main criterion for employment seems to be skill and had nothing to do with caste or religion.

★Takeaways: Peaceful coexistence can be achieved when Empathy is tempered by Rationality and sweetened by mere pinches of Acceptance and Compassion.

Chapter 7
Warfare & Intelligence

These aspects are also a specialty of Shivaji's style of working. Shivaji Maharaj had a small but effective standing army and was aware of its limitations. He knew he could not take on the big, well trained cavalry & field artillery of the Mughals in pitched battles. So he mastered guerilla tactics and repeatedly defeated the armies sent against him. He targeted their weakest point which is the supply lines and cut them off. He lured these armies into hills and jungles catching them at a disadvantage and attacking with various tactics like ambushes, sweeps, sudden raids and psychological warfare. This technique came to be known as *Ganimi Kawa* in Marathi language. All of this was backed up by his Intelligence unit. Shivaji had an extensive network of spies which brought him intelligence from within and outside the kingdom. A thorough intelligence briefing was done before taking any action. Unfortunately, very little is known about it apart from his Chief of Intelligence, Bahirji Naik. Bahirji was from the Ramoshi caste and frequently helped Shivaji in formulating strategies. Not being widely known is perhaps the very success of any intelligence unit.

★Takeaways: It is possible to defeat a much stronger enemy like David defeated Goliath, if you're smart, persistent and willing to do what is needed. Also, it is better to have some people with you who prefer to work in the shadows and are willing to forgo fame.

Chapter 8
Building a Navy to deal with the threat of Foreign Powers and Trade Policies

Shivaji Maharaj was the first to anticipate the threat of foreign invasion from the sea and the importance of having a naval fleet to protect the shore. He bought twenty *galivats* from the Portuguese. He inducted local people who were familiar with naval operations including the Malabar Pirates and Muslims. These people were from communities like *kolis, sonkolis bhandaris, etc.* but experienced in their field. One fleet was commanded by Daulat khan & the other by Admiral Maynak Bhandari.

As for trade policies, Shivaji had the foresight to protect local businesses by imposing heavy tariffs on foreign products. There is an entry of a letter sent by Shivaji to the Sarsubhedar of Kudal about levying heavy tax on foreign salt so that it is expensive than the local salt. There are other documents pertinent to the subject.

★Takeaways: We should be well rounded in our thinking to avoid stagnation. When all is going well we become complacent and can be caught on the wrong foot. And we should prefer local produce and products for our own economic growth.

Chapter 9
Abolition of Slavery

This is the most overlooked and underrated aspect of Shivaji Maharaj's career. We give credit to Abraham Lincoln for abolishing slavery with his Emancipation Proclamation in 1863 during the American Civil War. But Shivaji Maharaj had issued a charter to the Dutch in 1677 banning slave trade. The charter expressly warned the Dutch that they had to stop the slave trade. If they persisted, Shivaji Maharaj's people would stop them and take stringent measures. Shivaji was a ruler who thought about the well being of his people in every aspect.

★Takeaways: Respect for human dignity and promotion of liberty, equality & fraternity should be learnt from this event.

Some Humble Thoughts

All of achievements mentioned here are well documented with many more not mentioned. Shivaji Maharaj accomplished so much in such a short span of life. The basis for this was emphasis on Swaraj. Swaraj should be taken as a self-rule which is self-reliant & self-sufficient in the basics and beyond that. This has been a very exciting and humbling journey for me. It has inspired me to read more about this Extraordinary Man and I hope it spurs the readers to do the same. Hopefully, the fire of freedom in Shivaji Maharaj's eyes will be ignited in our hearts and minds as well.

Refences

Who was Shivaji (Shivaji Kon Hota) by Comrade Govind Pansare

Shivaji The Great Nation Builder by Government of Maharashtra, Directorate General of Information & Relations.

Beyond Borders: A Love That Defied Tradition

By Manmohan Sadana

I. A Meeting of Opposites

The monsoon rains poured over the bustling city of Pune, where the aroma of wet earth mixed with the distant scent of saffron-laced biryani. Inside the ancient walls of Shaniwar Wada, young warriors trained under the watchful eyes of their elders. Among them was Raghunathrao Bhosale, a skilled swordsman and the heir of a proud Maratha family. He had been raised on tales of valour, of Shivaji Maharaj's conquests, and of the duty that bound him to his ancestors.

On the other side of the city, in a home filled with the fragrance of sandalwood, Ameera Begum sat by the window, a book open on her lap. She was the daughter of a nobleman of Persian descent who had served the Bahmani Sultanate before the tides of history had shifted. Unlike the Marathas, her family valued poetry over warfare, diplomacy over battle, and faith over conquest.

Their worlds should never have collided. And yet, fate had other plans.

II. A Love in Secret

Their first meeting was at the home of a common acquaintance, a trader who dealt in silk and spices. Raghunathrao had come to negotiate the purchase of fine Persian carpets for his palace. Ameera had accompanied her father, curious about the warrior class she had heard so much about but never truly understood.

The moment Raghunathrao saw her, something shifted within him. She was unlike the women he had known— her eyes held stories, her voice was laced with wisdom, and her laughter carried a melody that lingered long after she had left.

For Ameera, the attraction was just as unexpected. She had been raised to believe that Marathas were men of war, hardened by battle, yet in Raghunathrao, she saw kindness, curiosity, and a desire to understand the world beyond his sword.

Their meetings became more frequent—stolen glances at gatherings, whispered conversations behind intricately carved screens, and letters exchanged under the pretense of poetry. With each passing day, love grew between them. But they both knew it was a love forbidden.

III. The Gathering Storm

News of their affection did not remain a secret for long. Raghunath Rao's uncle, Shivaji Pant, was a staunch traditionalist who saw marriage as a political alliance, not a matter of the heart. When he learned of his nephew's love for a woman outside their community, let alone of Persian lineage, his rage was boundless.

"This is treason against your own blood!" he thundered. "You are to marry a woman of your own people, someone who will strengthen our line, not dilute it with foreign ways!"

Raghunathrao met his uncle's fury with quiet defiance. "Love is not a battlefield, Kaka. It does not seek conquest. It seeks only to exist."

Meanwhile, Ameera's family was in turmoil. Her mother wept, fearing dishonor. Her father, usually a man of reason, was livid.

"You would abandon centuries of heritage for a warrior's son?" he demanded. "Do you not understand the cost?"

But Ameera did understand. She knew love came at a price.

IV. A Choice Between Duty and Heart

One evening, under the shade of a banyan tree, Raghunathrao and Ameera met in secrecy. He held her hands tightly, his voice heavy with emotion.

"Ameera, I will fight for us."

She shook her head. "You would fight your own blood for me? And what then? Even if we marry, we would be outcasts. You would lose your home, your people."

"I would rather lose everything than lose you," he vowed.

Tears welled in her eyes. "But I cannot bear to see you torn from your family, Raghunath."

The weight of their love was suffocating. They had defied expectations, but could they defy destiny?

V. A Love That Transcended Tradition

The confrontation between Raghunathrao and his family was inevitable. Before the entire assembly of elders, he declared his intention to marry Ameera.

"I am a warrior, yes, but I am also a man," he said, his voice steady. "And I will not let outdated traditions dictate whom I can love."

His uncle's face darkened. "If you go through with this, you are no longer a Bhosale. You will be cast out."

Ameera's family, too, refused to accept the union. "If you leave, you can never return," her father said.

Despite the warnings, Raghunathrao and Ameera chose love over lineage. With the help of a few trusted friends, they left Pune under the cover of night, seeking refuge in a distant kingdom where neither Maratha nor Persian rule dictated their fate.

They built a life together, away from the shadows of their past. In time, their love became a legend whispered among those who dared to challenge tradition. Some called them fools; others called them brave. But to each other, they were simply two souls who had chosen love over everything else.

VI. The Legacy of Love

Years later, when the dust of their defiance had settled, both families softened. Raghunath Rao's younger brother sent word that the family still thought of him, and Ameera's mother sent gifts for their children. Time, as it always does, healed wounds that once seemed irreparable.

Their love did not change history, nor did it erase the deep-seated traditions of their time. But it proved one thing—love, when true, knows no caste, no creed, no status, no religion.

Love is sublime.

(The above love story may be viewed with the following background in perspective):

"Where swords are raised and battles roar,
Where honour stands as iron's core,
There too beats a heart so true,
Bound by love in skies so blue.

The Maratha warrior, fierce and bold,
With tales of vallance often told,
Yet in the shadow of his might,
Lies a love that burns so bright.

For though his sword may carve the way,

His soul longs for a gentler stay,
Where hands so soft and eyes so deep,
Bid him rest and bid him weep.

His mother's voice, his sister's call,
His wife who waits behind the wall,
Not chains, but bonds of love so strong,
That guide his heart where it belongs.

And when the world demands his pride,
When duty pulls him far and wide,
He dreams of home, of laughter free,
Of love's warm touch beneath a tree.

No war can sever, no rule can break,
The love a Maratha vows to take,
For though the storm may shake the ground,
In love, his strength is truly found."

Revelations of the Deccan

By Anay Saxena

It had been a normal evening for most in the summer of 1680. The Indians had witnessed much upheaval in the preceding years. Shivaji, whose words had echoed through the ghats and vales, now lay on his deathbed. He recalled his humble beginnings, which had sprouted to turn into a tree of resistance against the Mughals. He wondered whether his life's work had been in vain or if the ideals he had fought for so dearly would become the source of inspiration for all mankind. His health had begun to decline, he took a deep breath, and his eyes closed.

He was awakened in the midst of vegetation, the chamber in which he had lain now surrounded by a century or so of decay and neglect. He looked around to see that the walls of the fort, which he had held so dear, had become a piece of history. The skies had not changed, though. Since he had fallen asleep, much had transformed.

The winds had become harsher, the temperatures had soared. Shivaji, under the unbearable heat, could only cover his head and march out of his deathbed. The scenery had not changed much, he thought. The fort, however ruined it may have been, still towered over the world. Those years of conflict had made Shivaji a stranger to the grandeur his fort embodied.

It looked desolate now; things seemed different, as if he had traveled a thousand years. As he walked through the ruined fort, looking at the gateways he had marched through or the grounds where his army had trained, all of it seemed familiar yet so strange. As his steps gained momentum, Shivaji's patrol turned into a brisk walk, similar to the walks he used to take in his heyday.

Then, a bright light flickered behind him for a short moment. Shivaji was alarmed, turning back instantly. "Who is there?" he said, shifting his left hand to his sabre's hilt. Shivaji turned to his left, then to his right. As the leafy floor slightly shook, Shivaji's eyes fixated on a young boy. The boy was not older than 20, wearing a strange set of clothes. His spectacles were oddly rectangular, and his hair kempt.

"Nice cosplay, dude!" the boy said, to the utter confusion of Shivaji. The king now stared at the lad as if he had been insulted. "What?" Shivaji muttered, as his grip on his sabre's hilt tightened. "What do you mean by 'what'? Are you not from here? You look EXACTLY like Shivaji, even the clothes look eerily similar," the boy replied, holding an odd rectangular slab of metal in his hand.

He continued, "Where did you get this stuff? You don't seem to find this anywhere, not online, not in the bazaars. Did you steal this from a museum? I'm going to call the police!" Shivaji could not comprehend what the lad was saying but felt that the boy was not a threat and thus loosened his grip.

"What exactly is this boy talking about?" Shivaji pondered, caressing his beard as he tried to make sense of the boy's utterly informal tongue. The king continued, "Who are you? Why do you stumble into the imperial grounds of Raigad?" The boy was amused and began laughing at his regal encounter.

"You were really immersed in this role, weren't you?" the boy said, now doing something on that metal slab in his hand. As he continued, the metal slab flashed a bright light for a few seconds. Shivaji was taken aback. How had he created light without fire?

"Dude, I don't know what you wanted, but you should probably go back to wherever you came from. It was getting late, and it would be closed to the public for the rest of the day. Come back tomorrow if you were really invested in this Shivaji ordeal."

"Wait, better idea! Since you looked so much like Shivaji, how about you started making this a gig? I mean, if there was a shortage of money, that is. Tourists dug that stuff, dude. You would be making so much money out of tourists, you would probably be as rich as the real Shivaji."

Shivaji was confused beyond comprehension. Why was Raigad fort being closed? It was the evening, and why was it ruined? And what did this boy mean when he blabbered on about tourism? The people were always free to consult the emperor. Shivaji slumped to the ground, still weak from his last encounter with death some 340-odd years ago. The boy rushed to his aid, and Shivaji's eyes faltered once more.

Shivaji woke up once more in a hospital, surrounded by a blinding white interior, with a solemn quiet and a hint of hustle and bustle. His regal attire was no longer with him, his sword lay on the table, and the boy was seated beside him. "Where am I now?" Shivaji said, his voice shaking, indicating his obvious irritation with it all.

"You were at the hospital; apparently, you were really sick. Why were you out there with dysentery?" the boy asked. Shivaji was still confused. The hospital had a distinct smell, and Shivaji did not like it one bit. He sneezed once, twice, a thousand times.

Shivaji said, "The emperor does not yield to diseases, and neither should any citizen." The boy was confused. "Brother, you're not Shivaji. Stop trying."

Shivaji finally shouted, "For the love of God and all that is holy, I am Shivaji! Why do you doubt me? I built my empire from dust and shook the foundations of Mughal rule! I'm not a poser, whatever you think I am. I am a Maratha king!"

The boy was taken aback but also became increasingly wary of this fellow walking around Raigad fort whom he happened to cross paths with. "I am Rohan, how do you do, Shivaji?" the boy said, formally introducing himself to a person whom he believed to be a poser.

"I'm Shivaji, as I've already said for the past few hours," Shivaji said, irritated but lethargic. He looked through the window as his gaze fixated on the greenery of the sloped Ghats. He remembered the casualties he had inflicted upon the Mughals and the Sultans of the Deccan. It seemed so distant to him now, being a product of a time of great instability. Now, he was surrounded by terribly bright walls, and a boy in unfamiliar attire sat beside him. The fort he had built with such pride lay in ruins.

Really, what had happened? Had the great Maratha emperor ultimately lost? Shivaji was confused, irritably so. "I think you should rest here for a week, I'll visit," Rohan said as he called the nurse to keep an eye on the historical figure.

And so the saga began. Rohan visited Shivaji every day of the week, and the lad found himself unknowingly in favor of the Maratha emperor. He found it amusing how dedicated one was to a role, despite him "accepting" that to the supposed king.

Finally, Shivaji found himself healed, and he was now free from the hospital's cages. Rohan took him on a little tour around his home when Shivaji told him that he had nowhere to go other than Raigad. Hence, Shivaji found himself wandering the streets of Mumbai with a boy he had known for not more than a week.

Shivaji was thoroughly impressed by the towering buildings. "The British achieved this?" he asked, to which Rohan replied, "The British? No, they haven't even been in Mumbai for 78 years." Shivaji was confused. The British had been a lowly force in India during his time, who had been at odds with Shivaji in the earlier segments of his reign.

The only thing that surprised Shivaji, of course, was the fact that the British, a lowly trading power, had been able to build such a magnificent city. He had held this notion until he saw the slums and garbage. "They didn't clean this up? I don't remember anything like this back in Delhi." Rohan laughed, "The Indian government is truly something, isn't it? It was 2025, and they hadn't a clue."

Shivaji was now even more clueless. How had his deathbed transported him 300 years into the future? He was now certain that his return to the Maratha throne would only have a negative effect. They had accepted that he had died; now he should live out his life in a city he once thought was backwater.

"Say, what has changed since my death?" Shivaji asked Rohan, who was now even more confused than the former. "Say what?" Rohan asked, chuckling. Shivaji insisted on what he had said, and Rohan was forced to comply. "Well, the Mughals collapsed after Aurangzeb's death in 1707—"

A grin civilized Shivaji's face, knowing that the Mughals had met an untimely end. "But then the Marathas turned into a confederacy. So most of India was decentralized."

"Not to mention the massacres. Yeah, a lot of the Maratha campaigns were brutal. Some Bengalis still hate them for that." Now Shivaji was intrigued, but before he could continue bombarding Rohan with his queries, the latter continued.

"Then the British captured Bengal, a lot of wars between them and the Marathas, which ultimately resulted in the destruction of Raigad fort and the conquest of India at the hands of the British—"

Shivaji threw his fists in the air, extremely displeased with the outcome of his descendants. "No-no, we got our independence almost two hundred years later though, so you shouldn't be THAT worried," Rohan added on, but Shivaji was still angry with the fact that his people had been enslaved for two centuries. Rohan started to hesitate before speaking, knowing that Shivaji was getting even angrier.

"We did get independence, though. S-so that's a positive, right?" Rohan stammered. Shivaji just stared at him.

"Okay, uh—then we've just been surviving till date? If that makes you feel happy?" Shivaji was not amused with Rohan's telling of history and stormed off. "Hey, where are you going? Come back here!" Rohan called out.

Shivaji stopped at the gates of a random park, went in, and sat on the grass. Rohan followed him and sat next to him.

"I heard of an emperor once. He reigned from his capital in Bihar, and his empire extended from Kalinga to Gandhara. I don't remember much about him, just that he was one of the greats. A man who truly knew how to rule," Shivaji said, tightening his fists. "He ruled as if the world needed him, ignoring the irrelevance of life. And in doing so, he found himself enriching the world around him."

"Ashoka?" Rohan asked.

"I don't know his name, but Ashoka is a fine and regal name. I wouldn't doubt a man of such stature to be named so aptly," Shivaji claimed. "I apologize for storming off like that. A man as invested in politics and nationalism as me not being furious over my countrymen being enslaved would be an appalling sight."

"I don't blame you. That part of history is in the past, though, no? We should learn to forgive but not to forget. There are bigger problems that we are to face," Rohan said as he played with the blades of grass, twirling them around.

"I am so utterly bored with it all," Shivaji said as he lay down. "Whatever the state of affairs, the people I fought for live free. And to me, that's all that matters."

Rohan smiled, knowing that this oddly-patriotic cosplayer was trying to open up to him. Not accepting the fact that the man he was talking to was actually a product of the seventeenth century, Rohan continued talking with his friend.

Shivaji continued on about his views on the new world around him, and Rohan introduced him to more information. Shivaji found himself learning from a boy whom he now considered to be his friend.

"You know, you're not that bad. I would have decapitated you if you had startled me even more the day we met. Perhaps, this world is not so shabby after all," Shivaji told Rohan as he fell asleep. His eyes closed once more, and now, everything went dark.

About the Authors

Kajari Guha, a poet, writer, translator, and composer, and winner of the Ukiyoto International Children's Book Awards, is a regular contributor to the anthologies published by Ukiyoto. Her books *Euphoric Vendetta: A Thriller*, *Pink, Rick, and Pip... The Scuba Divers*, *Pink, Rick, and Pip... The Birthday Guests*, and *Pink, Rick, and Pip... Their Adventure* have made a mark in the literary world.

***

Aurobindo Ghosh, a versatile personality with an M.Sc., M.Phil., and Ph.D. in Statistics, as well as a Ph.D. in Economics, is a teacher, trainer, and research guide. His first poetry book, Lily on the Northern Sky, won an award from Ukiyoto Publishing. He is a regular contributor to Ukiyoto Publishers' anthologies. His solo fiction book, Bimladadi's Dreams, also published by Ukiyoto, was not only awarded the 'Best Fiction Book of the Year' but was also adapted into an audiobook. His other solo works, Mystical Honeymoon, Deception Redefined, and Chronicles of Detective Subroto Deb Barman, are also published by Ukiyoto Publishing. Additionally, he creates acrylic, Warli, and Madhubani paintings.

***

Devajit Bhuyan, an electrical engineer by profession and a poet at heart, is proficient in composing poetry in both English and his mother tongue, Assamese. He is a fellow of the Institution of Engineers (India) and the Administrative Staff College of India (ASCI), as well as a life member of Asam Sahitya Sabha, the highest literary organization in Assam — the land of tea, rhinos, and Bihu.

Over the past 25 years, he has authored more than 80 books, published by various publishers in over 45 languages. His total published works across all languages amount to 210 and continue to grow each year. His writings are also part of the Class X curriculum under the Board of Secondary Education, Assam.

Among his published works, around 40 are Assamese poetry books, 30 are English poetry collections, four are children's books, and about 10 cover various other topics. Devajit Bhuyan's poetry explores a vast spectrum — from humans to animals, stars to galaxies, oceans to forests, humanity to war, technology to machines, and everything that exists on Earth and beyond.

He was honored as the Poet of the Year at the Assam Poetry Festival in 2022 and at the Kolkata Literary Carnival in 2023. He holds the unique distinction of being the only poet in India to release 34 poetry books in a single day at a single event.

To know more, visit: *www.devajitbhuyan.com*.

Priyadarshi has authored the non-fiction "आत्म-संदेह" and its English translation "Self doubt." As a dedicated artist and writer who brings a wealth of knowledge and passion to his work.

***

Dr. Priyanka Joshi, a History professor from Pune, has taught Maratha history for 12 years, authored academic and fiction books, and inspires students with Chhatrapati Shivaji Maharaj's wisdom and leadership.

***

Rohan Narvekar is a BAMS graduate practicing Ayurvedic Medicine for the past nine years. He has published one previous book.

***

Manmohan Sadana, a retired Joint Director General (Tourism) Government of India is an author, editor, actor and a mandolinist, whose novel – "Healing Strings" has won various awards which include the "Literary Titan Gold Award", "Golden Book Award", "Ukiyoto Emerging Author Award", "Certificate of Appreciation from Kerala Tourism Mart Society" and "Ukiyoto Book of the Decade Award". He has written many short stories which have been published in different anthologies and books. After superannuation from Government Service, he was a student of Persian for three years in St. Stephen's College, New Delhi and presently he is brushing his theatre skills as a student of renowned Director, Activist and Playwright, Mr. Arvind Gaur, in Triveni Kala Sangam, New Delhi.

***

Anay Saxena has been writing stories since the age of 7. Now aged 14, he continues to embark on his literary journey.

www.ingramcontent.com/pod-product-compliance
Lightning Source LLC
LaVergne TN
LVHW041542070526
838199LV00046B/1801